MARY CASSATT

MARY CASSATT

Portrait of an American Impressionist

Tom Streissguth

CAROLRHODA BOOKS, INC./MINNEAPOLIS

My thanks to Serge Leduc of the Musée d'Orsay, Paris, and to Monsieur Brignon of the Moulin Vert, Mesnil-Théribus, Oise, France, for their help in the preparation of this book.

Carolrhoda Books, Inc., c/o The Lerner Publishing Group
241 First Avenue North, Minneapolis, MN 55401 U.S.A.
Website address: www.lernerbooks.com

Library of Congress Cataloging-in-Publication Data

Streissguth, Thomas, 1958–
    Mary Cassatt : portrait of an American impressionist / Tom Streissguth.
        p.   cm.
    Includes bibliographical references and index.
    Summary: Presents the life and work of Mary Cassatt, the only American artist included with the French Impressionists.
    ISBN 1-57505-291-1 (alk. paper)
    1. Cassatt, Mary, 1844–1926—Juvenile literature. 2. Artists—United States—Biography—Juvenile literature. 3. Impressionism (Art)—Juvenile literature. [1. Cassatt, Mary, 1844–1926. 2. Artists. 3. Women—Biography. 4. Painting, American. 5. Art appreciation.] I. Title.
N6537.C35S76 1999
760' .092—dc21   98-7384
[B]

Manufactured in the United States of America
1 2 3 4 5 6 – JR – 04 03 02 01 00 99

CONTENTS

1. First, to France. 6

2. An Artist in Training 14

3. Study in France 22

4. A Professional Artist 30

5. The Impressionists. 40

6. An Independent Painter 58

7. Printmaking. 74

8. A More Traditional Challenge 84

9. Fame and Honor 92

Important Impressionist Artists 105

Where to See the Paintings. 107

Bibliography 109

Index 110

Acknowledgments. 112

1

First, to France

The clouds swirled over the North Atlantic Ocean, moving with the rain and wind and a small, eastbound passenger ship. On the upper deck, Mary Cassatt held tight to the wooden rails that kept her from sliding off the ship into the sea. Her father stood at her side, the two of them swaying as the ship moved up and down, a little to the left, much more to the right, down, up, down, up, left, right, left. . . . She felt sick.

Mary liked to walk along the decks and look across the waves to the eastern sky. Each morning, the sunrise would streak the sky with deep reds and oranges; then the clouds would turn from yellow to gray and white. The sea was like a beautiful painting that changed every day, sometimes every hour. In a few days, she knew, a strip of green land would appear over the horizon, and then a busy, noisy, gray, smoky English port. The Cassatts were going to stay in England for a few weeks and then take another boat across the English Channel to France.

In 1851 Mary Cassatt and her family sailed across the Atlantic Ocean to Europe. Mary liked to watch the colors of the ocean and sky change with the weather.

It was 1851, and Robert Cassatt was sailing overseas with his wife, Katherine, his sons Alexander, Robert, and Gardner, and his daughters Lydia and Mary. Seven-year-old Mary was closest to her brother Robbie, who was only two years older. Aleck was five years older than Mary, and Lydia seven. And Gard was five years younger.

The Cassatts were used to moving. Since May 22, 1844, when Mary Stevenson Cassatt had been born in a house on Rebecca Street in Allegheny City, Pennsylvania, they had moved three times to new homes. First they had moved from Allegheny City, where Robert Cassatt had been mayor, to nearby Pittsburgh. Then they had moved to a big country house called Hardwick, near the town of Lancaster, Pennsylvania. In 1849 the Cassatts moved into a big brick house on West Chestnut Street in Philadelphia.

Robert Cassatt had earned a good living as a banker and as a stockbroker. For twenty years, he had run his investment company, Cook & Cassatt. Although he was a newcomer to Philadelphia, he enjoyed high status in a city where people respected families with money and with a good background. His family had lived in New York, New Jersey, and Pennsylvania ever since Robert's great-great-great grandfather, Jacques Cossart, had sailed from France to the New World in 1662. Denis Cassat, Robert's father, had died bankrupt. But Robert, who changed his name to Cassatt, had invested wisely and had filled the Cassatt homes with fine rugs, old books, and expensive furniture. Robert Cassatt also owned several portraits of his family, all of them excellent likenesses.

But Mr. Cassatt didn't want to be a stockbroker or a banker anymore. He wanted to go to Europe and show it to his family. Life in Europe was inexpensive, and families like the Cassatts could afford to travel there and enjoy a life of ease and pleasure for as long as they wanted. The Cassatts would settle in Paris, the capital of France, where they could stroll in the parks and streets and visit the nearby palace of Versailles, the banks of the Seine River, and the Cathedral of Notre Dame. In Paris, Robert Cassatt had heard, life was to be enjoyed. The restaurants served good food and wine, there were theaters and art galleries to visit, and the shops sold the finest clothing in the world.

Mr. Cassatt also believed that Europe would be a good place to take his children. Studying the ancient buildings and monuments would teach them some history, and living in French society would teach them good manners. They would discover more about art, theater, music, and a different culture. The children would get along fine— Mary had already studied French in school—and Mr. Cassatt could send his sons to professional institutes in whatever field interested them.

After the Cassatts docked on the coast of France, Mr. Cassatt hired a coach to bring them to the capital. In Paris, the family moved into the Hotel Continental and then rented a furnished apartment. Mr. Cassatt hired the necessary servants and arranged for the education of his sons and daughters at private schools. Mary would continue her French lessons with a tutor. Here she could ride horses in a big park called the Bois de Boulogne. Here she could see as many paintings as she liked.

Mary had seen right away that Paris and Philadelphia were completely different. At home, their house was made of red brick; here the buildings were of gray or white stone, with steep roofs of black slate. On the bottom floors there were heavy tall doors with huge brass knobs and ropes that pulled bells inside. The doors led into mysterious courtyards, where horses and coaches stood waiting. The windows on the upper floors were narrow and opened out like pairs of doors onto tiny balconies or narrow terraces. There were no lawns anywhere, just a few small parks and fancy gardens surrounded by iron fences. Houses and shops crowded the edges of the sidewalks. Many old streets had no sidewalks or trees at all.

Mary took long walks through the big city. The streets were bustling with people and traffic. There was a lot of noise, and the echoing stone walls and cobbled streets seemed to make things even louder. There were a few well-dressed and wealthy people to be seen; others were merchants or workers. Most people talked in a hurry, waving their arms and using exaggerated expressions. Mary listened closely, if she could do it politely. She could usually understand what people were talking about, and she never had to guess their emotions.

There always seemed to be something very important going on. The newspapers carried dramatic stories about politics, the army, and the government. Mary often saw her father carefully reading the newspapers. On one memorable day—December 2, 1851—soldiers on foot and on horseback filled the streets. Robert Cassatt had been out for his usual morning walk but quickly came running back upstairs into the apartment, out of breath. "Well, Louis has done it!" he announced. The Cassatts went to the windows and looked out at the spectacle below.

Louis-Napoléon, the nephew of the late emperor Napoléon Bonaparte, was taking over the government of

France. Shots rang out; powerful cannons boomed down the avenues. Soldiers marched while people hurried from one place to another.

In the next year, Louis-Napoléon would proclaim himself the new emperor, Napoléon III. His government would control the newspapers, put many people in jail, and carefully watch the citizens with an army of secret police. Napoléon III would even dictate public taste. Following the lead of the new emperor, there would be new popular styles in clothes, literature, music, and art. Nothing like that would ever happen in Philadelphia!

The Cassatts stayed on in Europe, living on the income

Mary *(center)* and her brother Gard watch the painter, Peter Baumgärtner, as he sketches them, while Robbie plays chess with his father.

from Robert Cassatt's investments. Mr. Cassatt wanted his children to experience France and Paris, but he also wanted them to get a good education. In the spring of 1853, he decided to move the family to Germany. There Alexander could attend a much better school, one that prepared him for a career as a civil engineer.

For a time, the family lived happily in Darmstadt, in western Germany, where Alexander attended a technical university. The Cassatts journeyed in the countryside and walked through Heidelberg and Frankfurt. Mr. Cassatt also commissioned a new family portrait by an artist named Peter Baumgärtner. Mary studied German, which she learned to speak as well as she spoke French, and she took drawing lessons. But in early 1855, Mary's brother Robbie grew seriously ill. He had been suffering from a painful bone disease for several years, and the illness took a turn for the worse. On May 25, he died. The family could not bring his body back to the United States, so they had to bury him in Germany.

Robbie's death changed everything for Mary Cassatt and her family. Europe looked sad and gloomy, and it seemed too far from home. They left Alexander to finish his last year of studies in Germany while they returned to France.

In Paris they stopped to visit a fair called the Exposition Universelle. The exposition displayed all kinds of new-fangled scientific inventions as well as works of art. There were paintings by important French artists, including the famous and wealthy Eugène Delacroix. One painter whose works were not admitted, Gustave Courbet, exhibited in a different building. While Delacroix painted

Back in Paris, Mary went to the Exposition Universelle in the Palais de l'Industrie.

PALAIS DE L'INDVSTRIE

popular, huge pictures of famous events in history, Courbet painted ordinary scenes of the modern world, of nature, and of people at work or in their homes. Many people disliked Courbet's paintings.

Mary saw both exhibitions, but she wouldn't be seeing more. Mr. Cassatt did not want to stay in Paris. He remembered good friends and important business associates he had left behind in the United States. The children missed their old home and the hills where they used to play and ride horses. Later in 1855, four years after they first crossed the ocean, the Cassatts took another ship across the Atlantic and moved back to Pennsylvania.

2

AN ARTIST IN TRAINING

After returning from Europe, the Cassatt family moved into a house in West Chester, Pennsylvania, near their cousins. They lived in West Chester for three years and then moved into a large brick house in Philadelphia. In 1857 Aleck started courses at the Rensselaer Polytechnic Institute in New York, a fine engineering school. Mary finished high school in the spring of 1861, when she was seventeen years old.

Instead of literature, mathematics, or history, drawing had been Mary's real study. In her free time, she worked on pencil or charcoal sketches inside her house and outside on neighborhood streets. She was beginning to understand the secrets of showing the complex, three-dimensional world on a flat piece of paper or on canvas, the heavy white cloth used for oil painting. It was hard work to find the right lines and compositions, the arrangement of the objects in a painting. It was hard to solve the puzzling perspective, the spatial relationship of those objects, of even a simple landscape or interior scene. Painting itself, she discovered, was even harder. Different colors had to be arranged together in a certain way. Otherwise the effect was jarring—like a wrong note on a musical instrument. Success made her proud and happy; failure only made her more determined.

While still in school, Mary had decided that she would make a living on her own as a painter. After graduating from high school, she had to spend a long time working up enough courage to break the news to her father. She would have to choose the right words and find him in the right mood. She knew he might not take it very well.

She would have to return to Europe. To learn to paint, that was where one must study, and the best way to study was to copy museum pictures and work in artists' studios in France, Spain, or Italy. She would learn from professional artists and meet other students. She would travel. Europe wasn't like Philadelphia; there were beautiful sculptures in the streets and squares. There were paintings displayed in the windows of small galleries and on the walls of vast cathedrals. People in Europe had art surrounding them—they talked about art like Americans talked about money!

Robert Cassatt was patient and understanding. He listened to his daughter. He knew that Mary had talent, but even so, talented young ladies should not be bothered with careers. They especially did not work as painters. Art could be a hobby they might try, but only when their real duties, as wives and as mothers, allowed them time.

Mary grew stubborn. She would go to Europe. She

had already been there and had seen paintings, museums, and churches—it was Robert Cassatt who had brought her there! But it had been six years since the family had returned from Europe, and Mr. Cassatt had to think things over carefully. One thing was certain: Mary couldn't go back right then. The Civil War between the North and the South had broken out that spring. As long as the war lasted, she would have to stay safe at home.

Mr. Cassatt wanted to do the best he could for his children. If Mary wanted to study art, then she should go to art school. Perhaps after she finished a four-year course, she would be ready to marry, settle down, and make a home of her own. She didn't need to go to Europe—she could stay home in Philadelphia. The Pennsylvania Academy of Fine Arts, one of the best art schools in the country, was just a few blocks away, right down Chestnut Street. After Mary finished at the academy, she could decide what to do. She agreed and enrolled in the fall of 1861.

Mary and the other students at the Pennsylvania Academy of Fine Arts followed a strict course of training, much like the training followed by students in Europe. For four years, art instructors showed them how to draw and paint. First, the students copied old statues, most of them classical works from ancient Greece or Rome, to learn the correct proportions of the human body. Ancient Greek and Roman artists had used ideal proportions, and to be a successful artist, the student had to get these proportions right. In a drawing studio, with an instructor strolling among the students and looking over their shoulders, they copied faces, profiles, and the parts of the body:

During the Civil War, students at the Pennsylvania Academy of Fine Arts made flags for the Union Army.

trunks, arms, legs, feet, hands. They studied anatomy at lectures and made plaster casts of heads and the body at rest and in motion. They carefully drew from models, clothed or nude, who held long poses in front of the class.

After this preparation, students were allowed to copy paintings at the Philadelphia Museum of Art. They worked in the galleries, where Italian, Dutch, and French paintings served as examples of the correct way to compose pictures and to blend colors. By carefully following these examples, the students would learn how to design a painting in the "academic" way.

According to this training, poses had to be natural and proportions must be correct. The size of the painting must match its theme. Still lifes—pictures of inanimate objects, such as flowers or fruit—had to be small. Historical scenes were large. Portraits were about life-size.

Students also had to design their pictures correctly—the composition of a painting followed certain rules. Larger figures should be put near the center, and smaller ones toward the edges. The distance from the viewer to the subject could not be too close or too far.

The selection of colors was also very important. Darker hues—browns or even black—served in the background, with lighter colors highlighting the figures. Brighter hues of green, yellow, and red were to be used carefully in small areas. Finally, the strokes of the paintbrush should be invisible. The lines and curves of the design should disappear completely underneath the smoothly blending colors.

Only certain subjects were fit for painting. Students studied these subjects in school and would continue to use them throughout their careers. Art students could illustrate important events in history or episodes from ancient Greek and Roman mythology. They could paint portraits, landscapes, or still lifes.

According to academic training, artists should not experiment with the rules or engage in social commentary in their art. The artist's own feelings were not as important as his or her skill with color and design. Paintings served a purpose: they were intended to inspire fine feelings, to elevate the viewer above life's everyday problems and ordinary sentiments.

The art instructor, and eventually the art-buying public, judged the students on how well they carried out these many tasks. After finishing the academic course, a student would go out into the world and build a reputation on his or her ability to paint according to popular styles. If a painter followed instructions learned at the academy, he or she would be hired to paint portraits or scenes, win competition prizes, arrange prestigious solo exhibitions, and earn a living nearly as good as that of the buyers.

Mary Cassatt and the other female students at the academy followed the same course as the men. But the only male nude models they saw were plaster casts or statues, and the female students were expected to paint only certain subjects. Women were supposed to paint what they knew: family portraits, perhaps, or still lifes to decorate the dining rooms of their homes. Very few women became professional artists. Instead, women were supposed to graduate from art school and continue their painting or sculpture in their spare time, as a hobby.

Mary spent four years at the Pennsylvania Academy of Fine Arts, gradually tiring of the rules, repetition, and strict instruction. She dutifully attended anatomy classes and life-drawing classes, and copied the small collection of European and American paintings in the Philadelphia Museum of Art. The classes gradually became a boring

Students, including Mary *(far right)* and her friend Eliza Haldeman *(far left),* make a plaster cast of a man's hand. Behind them is a cast of Ghiberti's doors, *Gates of Paradise.*

routine, without interest or challenge. Her instructors, she eventually realized, could teach her nothing new; they could only judge her work by their set rules and standards.

Mary was sure there was much more to learn in Europe. There were no great collections of paintings in the United States for her to study, and like many Americans, she believed the best art made its home in European museums. The Civil War was over, passenger ships were sailing across the Atlantic again, and many other art students were crossing the Atlantic to study in Paris and in other European capitals.

Soon after she left the Pennsylvania Academy in 1865, she again asked her father's permission to return to Paris. There she could live with friends and set up her own painting studio. Even though she was nearly twenty-one years old—old enough to make her own decisions—Robert Cassatt was not happy at the thought of his daughter moving so far away. "I would almost rather see you dead!" he once exclaimed while arguing with her. She had finished school, and this, he believed, was the time to marry and settle down.

But Mary was determined to leave. Any serious artist had to study in Europe! Finally Robert Cassatt agreed to let her go and to give her a small allowance. With her mother, Mary sailed again for France late in 1865.

~ 3 ~
STUDY IN FRANCE

Paris had changed since Mary Cassatt had seen the city as a young girl. Under orders from Napoléon III and Baron Georges Haussmann, armies of masons and carpenters had torn down the old neighborhoods and the narrow, twisting streets to make way for long, straight avenues called *boulevards*. Haussmann sought to rid Paris of its unhealthy slums, and Napoléon believed the wide boulevards would enable his troops to easily fire cannons on any barricades or rioters.

Katherine Cassatt helped her daughter settle in to this beautiful city and, after a few months, returned to Philadelphia. With her best friend, Eliza Haldeman, who had studied with her at the academy, Mary strolled down the new boulevards, which ran through the center of the city and into the neighboring towns that had become part of the capital. New buildings were rising all over Paris, many of them tall, elegant apartment buildings with small iron balconies lining each floor. There were spacious parks, glorious monuments, and gaudy train stations that linked the city to the rest of France and Europe.

The boulevards seemed to create an entirely new society of their own. This was a leisure class of *bourgeois,* or middle-class, ladies and gentlemen known as the *boulevardiers.* They had time for strolling and enough money to enjoy restaurants, theaters, and private art galleries. They searched continually for amusement and for beautiful paintings to decorate the halls and rooms of their apartments and country homes.

But life could still be hard for artists. If painters weren't already wealthy, they had to sell several large paintings every year and accept young students into their studios in order to make enough money to survive. Many talented artists lived in tiny garrets—rooms just under the Parisian roofs that were usually inhabited by household servants. Most artists lived on meager diets, saving most of their money for paints, canvases, and the small fees they paid their models.

There was one sure measure of success for these painters: a good showing at the huge competition known as the Paris Salon. Every year, painters all over France sent their best works to the Salon, which held its exhibition in the Palais de l'Industrie. The Salon judging was almost like a religious ritual. After workers unpacked and set out the paintings in crowded rooms and hallways, the quiet and solemn Salon judges strolled between the

At the Paris Salon, Parisians gather to view the paintings crowding the walls.

works, giving each a quick glance. They awarded more than a thousand paintings the honor of hanging on the high, long walls of the Palais de l'Industrie for display to the public. But they rejected thousands of others, and only one painting each year won the highest honor, the Prix de Rome. Nevertheless, every serious artist in France took part, because success at the Salon ensured sales of their paintings to private buyers.

Mary Cassatt joined the crowds of fashionable Parisians who visited the Palais de l'Industrie to examine the paintings accepted at the Salon. Although the paintings had already passed through a rigorous examination, many of them still displeased the public. The colors seemed off, or the poses were not balanced, or the frames were too small or too gaudy. The pictures drew witty remarks, sarcastic commentaries, quiet laughter, and even a few murmurs of astonishment and admiration.

Someday, Mary knew, she would send one of her own works to the Paris Salon. Soon, she hoped, she would have something worthy of being examined by the Salon judges and even accepted. She could not go to the École des Beaux-Arts, the big art school in Paris, because women were not admitted there. But she soon had an important victory: she was accepted as a private student by Jean-Léon Gérôme, one of the best-known painters in France and in the world. She was also granted a permit to copy paintings in the Louvre, a huge old palace on the banks of the Seine River that held the biggest collection of paintings and sculpture in the world. Hundreds of young art students set up their easels in the Louvre to study color and composition. Professional copyists were paid to copy famous works for tourists who wanted to bring something home from their travels.

Mary also began working at the *atelier,* or studio, of a popular painter named Charles Chaplin. He followed the

Another American artist, Winslow Homer, drew the art students and copyists working at the Louvre in 1867.

academic style taught at the Pennsylvania Academy of Fine Arts and at the École des Beaux-Arts. Like many other well-established painters, he opened his studio to younger artists for study and practice. Mary arrived several times a week, with several other painters, to paint or sketch models in the atelier, while Chaplin strolled about the studio and offered criticism, suggestions, or praise.

Study in an atelier was one of the best ways to learn painting. Mary and Eliza Haldeman both attended Chaplin's studio and soon became two of his favorite pupils. But Mary soon realized that Chaplin was a traditional artist who didn't have any new ideas to offer her.

In early 1867, after quitting Chaplin's, she and Eliza moved to the small village of Courances, near Paris. Here the two young artists could apply their ideas and training to subjects taken from real life. It was time to leave the closed environment of the classroom for the artistic inspiration of the real world.

In Courances, Mary and Eliza set up a studio in a small house. There they painted the villagers going about their daily lives—working in their homes or in the fields. The two artists were struck by the dignified behavior and graceful nobility of the French peasants, which contrasted with the more straightforward and brash manners of the American working class.

With the advice and guidance of Charles Chaplin, Mary and Eliza both sent paintings done in Courances to the Paris Salon of 1867. The judges rejected both works.

Mary still lived close enough to Paris to visit exhibitions whenever she wanted. One of the most important art shows took place during the Paris World's Fair of 1867, when the painters Gustave Courbet and Édouard Manet put on shows of their works in separate pavilions. Courbet and Manet, Mary soon discovered, hated academic painting. For them, the strict rules and confinement to familiar, mythological subjects robbed paintings of feeling. If there was no feeling, there was no real interest for the viewer, or so they believed. Instead, they created more realistic pictures, with subjects that interested or challenged them, taken from the real world. In his painting *Luncheon on the Grass,* Manet had even painted a nude woman in a modern setting—a picnic in the countryside—with the woman looking straight at the viewer. This was definitely against the rules! Critics and art buyers scorned this realistic style. But it fascinated Mary Cassatt.

Later in 1867, Mary and Eliza moved to another small village, Écouen, where a small colony of artists were painting the landscapes, scenes, and people that surrounded them. Both women studied with a local painter named Paul Soyer. They took small trips into the nearby countryside to sketch and paint, and traveled to the coast of Normandy to sketch fishing ports and the seaside. On one trip, Mary traveled south to the sunny hills of Provence and the windy mountains of Savoy, near the border of France and Italy. She saw the Mediterranean Sea and Mont Blanc, the highest mountain in France. She returned to Paris with her sketchbooks filled with views of the mountains and of the people she had seen.

In 1868 Mary and Eliza again sent paintings to the Paris Salon. And this time, they were accepted. Mary's picture was a simple portrait of a young girl playing a mandolin. The judges ordered that it be hung "on the line," or at eye level, where it would be easiest for visitors to see.

Mary was proud of this honor but wasn't sure how much of an honor it really was. The judges had accepted nearly three thousand paintings that year!

In 1870 war interrupted Mary Cassatt's studies again. That summer, Napoléon III's army began fighting Prussia, a German state. After war was declared on July 18, Mary and her mother, who had been visiting France, sailed back to the United States. While Mary had been in France, her brother Aleck had married Lois Buchanan, the niece of the former president James Buchanan. When Mary returned to Pennsylvania, she met her sister-in-law. The two strong women immediately disliked each other.

As the Prussians swept through northern and central France, Mary read about the Franco-Prussian War in the Philadelphia newspapers. For four months, Paris was under siege. Finally, Prussia defeated the French army and took Napoléon III prisoner. In 1871 a treaty was signed between the two countries. France had to give up some of its territory and pay Prussia five billion francs, or about one billion dollars, for losing the war.

The defeat humiliated and enraged the French people. In the spring of 1871, workers rioted in the streets of Paris. They set up barricades of lumber and paving stones and fought with police. The mob destroyed property and burned many buildings to the ground. The government called in the army; soldiers on horseback shot down rioters by the thousands. The Paris Salon was not held that year.

Mary had been working on several portraits in France. They were the first works she thought she might be able to sell, so she had brought them back with her to the United States. After spending four years at an art academy and four more years studying with teachers in France, she wanted to start making a living. She sent two of her pictures to an art dealer in New York City but found no buyers. With two of her cousins, she traveled to Chicago to show the paintings in another gallery. While they were there, on October 8, a tremendous fire broke out in the city. The fire destroyed nearly every building in Chicago's downtown, including the gallery. Mary escaped the fire, but her paintings were burned.

Mary returned to Pennsylvania, sad and discouraged. It seemed she had not accomplished much with all the years she had spent learning to paint. Perhaps she should stop trying, find a different career, and paint only as a hobby as a proper woman should. "I have given up my studio," she wrote to a friend, "and have not touched a brush for six weeks." Her father, she knew, would be happy to have her stay near the family's home in Pennsylvania. The dream of working as an independent painter would have to stay just a dream.

4

A Professional Artist

In the United States, there were few professional artists for Mary to talk to, and the familiar streets and countryside of Pennsylvania offered her no inspiration. But in 1871, two of her paintings did attract the attention of the bishop of Pittsburgh. He wrote to Mary, offering her a commission to copy religious paintings by an Italian artist named Correggio. The paintings were in the city of Parma, in northern Italy, and the bishop wanted the copies to decorate a new cathedral in Pittsburgh. Mary happily accepted the commission, which would pay three hundred dollars and, more importantly, allow her to return to Europe. With another skilled painter, Emily Sartain, Mary braved yet another ocean voyage.

This time, instead of stopping in France, she traveled directly to Italy. In Parma and in other Italian cities, painters of the fifteenth century had broken away from the religious painting traditions of the Middle Ages to create a style that was more worldly and realistic. The art

While she was in Parma, Italy, Mary experienced her first critical success.

took inspiration from the myths and literature of ancient Greece and Rome, which had been revived by the scholars and poets of the Renaissance, the great rebirth of European art and culture begun in the fourteenth century.

Parma had a stately *duomo,* or domed cathedral, where Mary could study the paintings and sculpture of skilled Renaissance artists. On the inside of the high dome, Correggio had painted a graceful Assumption scene. The painting showed the Virgin Mary ascending to heaven with the angels. In another room, the walls were covered by other Correggio works. After Mass was said and the congregation left their places, Mary could enter the duomo to sketch from the many paintings and frescoes, paintings made on fresh plaster. To finish the commission she had been given in Pittsburgh, Mary also spent many long days behind her easel in the Parma museum.

In the studio she had rented, Mary carefully re-created works she admired, trying to learn drawing and color directly from the Italian masters who had worked in these same cities centuries before her. By this time, she had adopted her own straightforward method of working. She always began with a simple drawing using a pencil or a small stick of charcoal. While working out ideas, she could erase the lines and change the basic design if she wanted. For a single painting, she might make dozens of sketches, trying to find the right way to show figures in the picture. A good painting had to have strong, interesting lines and shapes working within the drawing and underneath the color.

After finishing the sketches and studies of difficult parts of the picture, she would work out the drawing on a piece of canvas stretched tightly across a wooden frame. Then she mixed oil paints to color it. She carefully chose her colors. Certain colors were stronger than others; certain colors worked well together. Some colors she favored; others she avoided altogether. She hired a model to come to her studio and take the pose she had already worked out in the sketches and on the canvas. She didn't bother with a model until she knew exactly what the pose would be.

It took weeks and sometimes months of hard work to finish a painting. In time, Mary could find the best colors for her paintings. But the drawing within the painting always remained the most important part. If the drawing was poor, she could not make it better with agreeable color, precise brush strokes, or a pretty frame.

In the meantime, to work on her drawing technique, she took lessons in engraving from a local artist named Carlo Raimondi. Engravings were drawings made by pushing a sharp steel needle across the surface of a copper plate. After completing the drawing, the artist covered the plate with ink. The ink stuck to the surface of the plate but not to the lines or areas cut into the copper. The inked plate was then pressed against a sheet of paper to create a print. Many prints could be made from the same plate.

Painters studied engraving as a way to improve their drawing. Engraving took patience and skill—a false or clumsy line made with the engraver's needle could not be covered up, painted over, or erased. The composition had to be strong, and the artist's hand had to be sure and steady. In the hours when she had lost the daylight needed for outdoor sketching or painting, Mary would ink the copper plate and make prints by the faint light of the oil or gas lamps used in her studio.

In early 1872, Mary began working on a canvas called *On the Balcony.* She placed two women in the front of the picture. While one woman watches the street below, the other glances to the background, smiling and holding a fan over her shoulder. In the background stands a man in a dark suit and a wide-brimmed hat. The painting shows only his shadowy face, his white shirtfront, his hat, and a brightly lit hand gripping a wall.

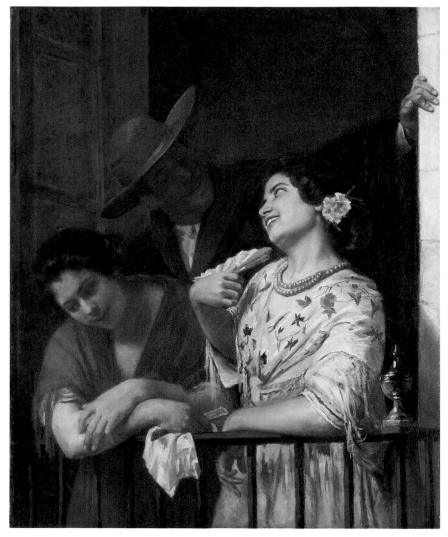

Mary's *On the Balcony*

Mary had done this picture in the familiar style of "balcony paintings." The Spanish artist Francisco Goya had painted a similar picture, and so had Édouard Manet, who had exhibited a painting called *The Balcony* at the Paris Salon in 1869. Proud of her picture, Mary sent it to

Édouard Manet painted *The Balcony* in 1869. His future sister-in-law, Berthe Morisot, is seated in front. Morisot later became a painter.

the Paris Salon of 1872. At that time, Spanish subjects were popular with the public and familiar to the Salon judges. They accepted *On the Balcony* and listed it in the thick exhibition catalog as Painting Number 1,433. Mary gave her name as "Mary Stevenson," using her middle name. She was pleased with her success but did not yet feel ready to exhibit her works under her family name.

In 1873 Mary traveled to Spain, where she lived for six months. She stayed for a time in Madrid, where she spent many afternoons walking in the long galleries of the Prado Museum. She studied the works of Diego Velázquez and Bartolomé Murillo. She set up an easel in the Prado to make a copy of a famous work by Velázquez and began several new paintings of her own.

In a train coach reserved for female passengers, Mary rode south to Seville, a city in the region of Andalusia. For five months, she painted in a studio in the Casa de Pilatos, an old Sevillian palace. She enjoyed her freedom as a visitor and an outsider.

Here she could paint what she wanted, instead of what teachers and other students expected her to paint. Several of her pictures were inspired by her surroundings in Spain and by bullfighting. One of these works is a portrait, in profile, of a young bullfighter. In another, a young woman offers a *panale,* a sweet drink, to the same *toreador.* While Mary was still living in Spain, she sent this painting, *Offering the Panale to the Toreador,* to the Paris Salon. The judges again accepted her work.

After her travels in Spain, Mary went north to Holland. She spent the summer copying and learning from the works of two seventeenth-century painters, Frans Hals and Peter Paul Rubens. While working in a gallery, she met a French painter named Léon Tourny. She and Tourny admired the paintings of Rubens and of other Flemish artists who had developed a strong, emotionally intense style of their own, much different from that of French or Spanish artists. While she was in Antwerp, Belgium, she also painted a portrait of her mother, who was visiting Mary in Europe.

When Mary returned to Paris, she again took up friendships with American and French painters. Having several works accepted at the Salon had won her respect among the city's many artists and art critics. She also met a younger American named Louisine Elder, a seventeen-year-old boarding school student.

On one of their walks, Mary and Louisine stopped at the window of a small gallery, where Mary saw a picture by the painter Edgar Degas. The work was a drawing in pastel, a chalky crayon that gave much softer colors and lines than oil paints. Degas had titled the picture *Ballet Rehearsal*. It showed a ballet master directing a group of his students, who practiced their difficult stances with confidence and ease.

Mary stood at the window for a long time, entranced by the drawing and by the beautiful light pastel colors. Degas had captured the complex motion of a ballet rehearsal with great skill. The figures in the drawing seemed to be alive and moving to unheard music through and around the frame of the picture. Such a simple scene from the familiar world inspired the viewer. It showed

In the early 1870s, Edgar Degas was taken with the complexity and form of ballet rehearsals and completed several paintings of them.

Mary that a good artist such as Degas could freely express his own personality through his work. All the rules of her academic training were, for a moment, forgotten, while an entirely new world of challenges and possibilities revealed itself.

Mary's enthusiasm for *Ballet Rehearsal* inspired Louisine Elder to buy it with all of her spending money: five hundred francs, or one hundred dollars. It was the first artwork that Louisine had ever bought.

With her acceptance at the Paris Salon, Mary Cassatt was becoming more widely known. The French public took a keen interest in the ability of a woman—an American at that—who could compete with the best painters of their own country.

In 1874 Cassatt sent a portrait called *Ida* to the Salon, and this time her real name appeared in the exhibition catalog. One of the many admirers of the painting was Edgar Degas. While strolling through the huge exhibition with his friend Léon Tourny, he stopped to take a long look at *Ida.* Finally Degas turned to Tourny and exclaimed, "There is someone who feels as I do!"

5

THE IMPRESSIONISTS

"I can not accept this illegitimate judgment of colleagues, whom I have not assigned the task of appreciating my work! I want my work to be exhibited to the public anyway. My wish does not seem the least bit exorbitant," wrote the French painter Paul Cézanne in 1866. He was unhappy with the judges of the Paris Salon, who had rejected one of his paintings. To Cézanne, the idea of an official contest between artists was absurd. The Salon would be ridiculous if it did not hold such control over which paintings were seen and bought by the public, and which artists became famous enough to make their living by painting.

Cézanne was not alone in his protest. Many other talented artists had displeased the painting judges by working out new styles that were unacceptable at the Salon. In

the 1860s, Degas had submitted *The Bathers.* Édouard
Manet had sent *Luncheon on the Grass,* the painting that
had scandalized the public by showing a nude woman at a
picnic. The Salon jury had rejected both works. Claude
Monet and Camille Pissarro weren't winning any prizes
either, as they would not paint according to academic
rules and styles. Although Cézanne had tried to establish
a separate Salon des Refusés (Hall of the Rejected) for
those who had not satisfied the juries, the idea failed.

In the first few years after France's defeat in the
Franco-Prussian War, when it seemed all of France was
engaged in an angry protest, Manet, Cézanne, Degas,
Monet, Pissarro, Auguste Renoir, Alfred Sisley, and
Berthe Morisot banded together to fight the academic art
world. They would work together, trade ideas, and
arrange exhibitions of their own. They would hold no
competitions and make no awards; they would find their
own public. They called themselves the "Independents."

The Independents were not interested in painting mythological or historical scenes. They drew no gods or god-
desses; they didn't care about Salon traditions. Like Mary
Cassatt, they painted the modern world, the one they saw
around them every day. Streets, gardens, homes, and their
own painting studios provided the background for their
works. Instead of heroes and angels, everyday people filled
their canvases: gardeners and maids, dancers, coach drivers,
farmers, and ordinary-looking mothers and children. The
Independents avoided dark shadows and somber colors.
They used a wide range of bright colors in all areas of their
canvases. Unlike the academic painters, they often left their

Camille Pissarro's *Boulevard Montmartre in Paris* shows the liveliness of an ordinary city street.

studios to work. They rode the new steam-powered trains to the distant countryside, where they set up small easels to paint forests, fields, village homes, and the seaside. Intent on a new realism in their pictures, they carefully rendered the changing effects of wind, clouds, and natural light.

But to the academic painters, the Independents simply couldn't paint. To the Salon judges, the Independents' subjects were vulgar and ordinary, their canvases too bright, and their drawing sloppy. Instead of carefully blending colors to make the brush strokes disappear, the Independents carelessly slapped paint onto the canvas.

The brush strokes were visible, the lines of the drawing were blurry, and the colors clashed. There was no logic, no order, and no taste. These Independents, the judges believed, were simply incompetent. Many art experts and critics compared their paintings to the work of children. A Monet painting called *Impression, Sunrise* prompted one critic, Louis Leroy, to sarcastically call these artists "Impressionists." Other critics and the public soon picked up the expression. The group of young painters who were fighting against the Salon, academic painting, and the jury system came to be called Impressionists.

Claude Monet's *Impression, Sunrise* gave the name to the Impressionist movement.

On April 15, 1874, two weeks before the start of the Paris Salon, the Independents opened their first public exhibition. The show took place at a photographer's studio on the Boulevard des Capucines. Large crowds of curious boulevardiers filled the studio to examine the works. Some left the studio grumbling angrily; others laughed or made disparaging remarks. A few painters and critics arrived to carefully examine the new approaches to drawing, color, and subject matter.

In 1874, although Cassatt had sent the portrait called *Ida* to the Salon, she had been away, traveling in Italy, and missed the Independents' first exhibition. When she returned to Paris that summer, she found that her friends were still talking about Renoir, Pissarro, Monet, Sisley, and their exhibition. Cassatt herself, after several years of work and study in Europe, was still feeling discouraged. She still was not selling any of her works. Her paintings seemed out of fashion; few buyers were interested in her toreadors and balcony scenes.

About the time of the Independents' first exhibition, she decided on a new course: she would paint portraits. She worked on several pictures of members of her own family. Her sister, Lydia, moved to France at the end of the summer. The next spring, Cassatt sent a portrait of her sister to the Salon. The judges rejected that painting but accepted a second one, a picture of a young girl.

Cassatt began to prepare another canvas for the Salon. The painting showed a woman knitting. The subject, shown against a brightly colored background, looked directly at the viewer and held a simple pose. This time, the Salon judges rejected her work. Painting and art were serious matters, and paintings—even of familiar objects and everyday life—must have dark backgrounds. Disappointed, Cassatt reworked the painting with a proper, more somber backdrop. The judges accepted it.

The rejection of her work had, at first, disappointed her. But when the judges accepted her picture only after she had changed the background to suit them, Cassatt grew angry. She realized that if she continued sending her works to the Salon, the system of juries, contests, awards, and official exhibitions would end by controlling her work. The judges, representing traditional art academies and popular taste, would dictate what to paint and how to paint it.

In her studio, and while walking along the busy boulevards, Cassatt spent time thinking about the problem. Success at the Salon would help her sell works in private art galleries and help her win a good reputation in the press. She might have orders for paintings, perhaps more orders than she could carry out, from wealthy patrons. But she wasn't going hungry and she didn't need commissions, certainly not if it meant painting in a manner she disliked. Instead, she decided, she would follow her own instincts and paint as she wanted. She believed that was the only way for an artist to improve and to create good work. Someday, she believed, her work would find a public on its own, without help from judges, juries, and painting contests.

After the Salon of 1874 closed, Cassatt won several commissions for portraits. Many came from Americans who wanted a portrait of themselves or their family as a

Mary Cassatt painted Louisine Elder's friend in *Mary Ellison Embroidering,* one of the portraits commissioned at this time.

souvenir of their visit to Paris. After finishing these pictures and turning them over to the buyers, Cassatt used her sketches and ideas for other paintings that she could sell herself or submit to the Salon. She still depended on her reputation as a Salon artist, which assured buyers and patrons that, in the world of traditional painting, she had been judged worthy.

The Independents, meanwhile, had cast off their connections to the Paris Salon. In order to publicize their works, they had to continue holding exhibitions of their own. Two more Independent shows were held in 1876 and 1877, but the shows were not a success. Critics writing for the newspapers and art journals made fun of the new style. Obviously, these painters couldn't paint—that was why they did not show at the Paris Salon. They could only dab at their canvases with odd colors. Instead of painting figures or scenes, they could only make "impressions."

Like any other group or artistic movement, the Impressionists soon had their leaders and followers. Edgar Degas, the artist of *Ballet Rehearsal,* was a leader of the Impressionists from the beginning. He had been brought up in a wealthy family and had lived well while studying painting as a young man. At first, he had no pressing need to sell his works or satisfy the public, so he felt free to explore a new style of painting on his own. Art critics and general opinion had little effect on him. Degas had many strong opinions, and he never hesitated to express them to his friends or to other artists. He could be helpful and encouraging, or humiliating, sarcastic, and exasperating. Even artists who earned his friendship and respect still feared his sharp tongue.

A brilliant artist, Edgar Degas saw each work as a challenge to his mind and to his painter's eye. He most enjoyed finding the solution to the problems that paintings posed: how to arrange the subjects, how to color them, and how to carefully balance lines and forms to create a good design. He loved to create complex compositions on the canvas; the dancers in a ballet class, or the figures of bathers at a washstand, provided ideal subjects for his sketches and paintings. His new approach to painting and to the composition of his pictures inspired Mary Cassatt to begin experimenting with difficult poses on her own.

One day, Degas decided to call on Mary Cassatt in her studio with his friend Léon Tourny, whom Cassatt had met a few years earlier in Holland. Degas had admired Cassatt's works at the Salon and believed her approach to painting suited the Impressionist movement. After examining the canvases and drawings in the studio, he invited her to join the Impressionists and to exhibit her works at their next show.

Cassatt quickly accepted the invitation, even though she knew that joining the Impressionists would brand her as a modern painter, a "rebel," and might even cost her commissions and sales. Critics would scorn her, and friends such as Emily Sartain, who stayed with traditional, academic painting, would drift away. But she didn't care. This group of artists accepted her as an equal. They might criticize and question her work, but in the end they would allow her a style of her own. She had the sensation of finally being able to breathe freely and paint the way she really wanted.

Degas and Cassatt became close friends. She had already heard much about him—Degas had been accepted at the Paris Salon many times and often held shows of his work at private galleries. Both painters were strong-willed and not shy about expressing harsh opinions of other artists and their works. Degas admired Cassatt's talent, but he especially liked her independence. He could talk to this American in a plain and honest manner that he would never use with French women, whom he always treated with the gallantry they expected of a bourgeois gentleman. He often gave Cassatt advice on her paintings. Once he helped her to paint the background to one of her pictures, *Little Girl in a Blue Armchair.* Mary Cassatt showed skill and good taste. She could also draw, a talent that Degas believed quite rare among women.

Cassatt's *Little Girl in a Blue Armchair*

Mary Cassatt planned carefully for her first show with the Independents. The shows were growing larger each year; for the third show in 1877 more than two hundred paintings by eighteen artists had been exhibited in a large, elegant apartment. In the summer and fall of that year, Cassatt spent many days strolling around Paris and sketching ideas for the paintings she would submit for the fourth show.

As could be expected for a group of independent artists, the Impressionist group was in turmoil. Some artists were leaving the group, while others sought to join only for the sake of publicity. Degas and the others also found that the 1878 International Exposition, which would take place in Paris, was attracting much of the public's attention away from art exhibitions. They decided to delay their next show until the following year.

Edgar Degas brought Cassatt into the Impressionists' inner circle and became one of her closest friends.

One of Degas's prints shows Cassatt standing as she examines paintings in the Etruscan Gallery of the Louvre.

Cassatt had one more year to prepare. By April 10, 1879, the first day of the exhibition, she had readied eleven paintings and drawings. They were all hung together in a single room—the first time she had displayed more than two of her paintings at any exhibition. Several notices appeared in the newspapers and art reviews, and more than sixteen thousand people saw the exhibition. Attracted by the controversy swirling around the group, a few visitors boldly made offers for paintings. The artists divided the profits from the show among themselves, and with the 440 francs she earned, Cassatt bought pictures by Degas and Monet.

Cassatt's works attracted some good reviews. Many critics compared her works to those of Edgar Degas.

Mary Cassatt's portrait of herself, painted in 1878, shows a confident artist who is at ease with her newly adopted style of painting.

For *Woman with a Pearl Necklace in a Loge,* Mary used her sister, Lydia, as her model. While Degas painted dancers on stage, Cassatt turned around and painted those sitting next to her. As one critic wrote: "There is nothing more graciously honest and aristocratic than her portraits of young women, except perhaps her *Woman in a Loge.*"

A critic named Arsène Hussaye wrote: "There isn't a painting, nor a pastel by M[ademoiselle] Mary Cassatt that is not an exquisite symphony of color. M[ademoiselle] Mary Cassatt is fond of pure colors and possesses the secret of blending them in a composition that is bold, mysterious, and fresh."

The hard-won acclaim gradually brought more buyers to Cassatt's studio. With several of her works selling at the annual Impressionist exhibitions and a new market growing among those who were bravely collecting Impressionist works, she could finally leave behind any worry of not succeeding as a professional artist.

Mary Cassatt didn't need the money her paintings earned to live and eat, as did many Impressionist painters. She lived with her mother and father and her sister, Lydia, since her parents had moved to Paris in 1877. The four Cassatts had rented an apartment on the sixth floor of a building on Avenue Trudaine, near the steep hill of Montmartre in the northern part of the city. With her earnings from her paintings, Mary could rent her own studio not far away, buy canvases and paints, and pay models to pose for her pictures.

Mary Cassatt was growing more confident that she could sell her works. In 1878 and 1879 she had exhibited paintings at the Pennsylvania Academy. She exhibited at the National Academy of Design in New York in 1880. Her paintings were the first Impressionist works to be displayed in public in her home country. Art dealers in Paris, as well as Philadelphia, were attracting buyers. Paul Durand-Ruel, a Parisian art dealer who specialized in Impressionist works, often called at Cassatt's studio to ask after paintings she might have available for sale.

Cassatt's paintings drew favorable notices in American newspapers, as well as the art journals of Paris. She was the only American to exhibit with the notorious Impressionists, yet she was also a trained professional who had studied at a traditional art school. Her work was not as strange and experimental as works by other Impressionists, and as a result, reviewers in both countries took her art seriously.

Although she exhibited with the Impressionists, Mary Cassatt treasured her independence and did not really see herself following or leading any art movement. Degas and the other painters she had joined inspired her with their free and more personal approach to painting, but Cassatt did not copy their style. She simply painted as she wished without worrying about labels that others might give her work.

The subjects Cassatt painted revealed her streak of independence. Many of her pictures showed women alone. She painted women in their gardens or in their homes. The outside world was kept far away; the worlds of work and of the city streets, and even of the respectable society to which the Cassatts belonged, were nearly invisible. Cassatt painted her subjects at comfortable, everyday activities: drinking tea, reading a newspaper, knitting, dressing, or holding infants. In one painting, the dignified Lydia drives a carriage with Degas's niece at her side. In another, *At the Opera,* a lady wearing elegant clothes uses spyglasses to watch an opera. She sits by herself in a private box, far from the stage and alone in the well-

Cassatt's *At the Opera*

dressed crowd. Dabs of paint show a few members of the audience who seem to be watching her from distant seats.

The viewer of Cassatt's paintings must guess at the emotions of the subjects. The men, women, and children

Cassatt's *Five O'Clock Tea*

in the paintings look away from the viewer, as if they had been caught in a private moment and in a private world. *Five O'Clock Tea* shows Mary Cassatt's sister, Lydia, and another woman seated at a tea table. Both figures pose on the left side of the painting and seem to avoid the center, where the viewer's attention would naturally focus. A tea service occupies the other side; a teacup hides the face of one woman, while the other stares off into the distance. The painting looks like a candid photograph, taken by chance and holding secrets known only to the artist and her subjects.

6

AN INDEPENDENT PAINTER

By 1880 Mary Cassatt was becoming one of the best-known painters in France. With the money she earned from selling her own works, she began to collect the paintings of artists she knew and admired. She helped her friend Louisine Elder, as well as her brother Alexander, who was enjoying a successful career as a railroad man, to buy canvases of their own. Mary's opinion of other artists mattered quite a bit more to them than the advice offered by gallery owners and other art promoters. With Mary Cassatt's advice, Louisine Elder and Alexander Cassatt became the first people in the United States to collect Impressionist paintings.

Cassatt held strong opinions of paintings as well as of people. She felt contempt for those who didn't live or work up to her standards, and her quick tongue often got her into trouble. Several times she argued bitterly with close friends, such as Emily Sartain or Eliza Haldeman,

Cassatt painted another self-portrait in 1880, again showing herself in a stylish hat.

and for long periods of time found herself not speaking to a certain painter, teacher, gallery owner, or art buyer. She often found herself unpopular with members of her own family, and she always seemed to have trouble with Aleck's wife, Lois.

Cassatt's *Portrait of Alexander J. Cassatt, and His Son, Robert Kelso*

In 1880 Aleck had brought his family to Paris for a long holiday. He stayed in the capital for several weeks, visiting his relatives living in France. Aleck enjoyed wandering through art galleries; like his father, he had a taste for French art, food, and culture. Everybody enjoyed themselves and their Aunt Mary, except perhaps for Lois Cassatt, who was certain that her husband was throwing his hard-earned money away on worthless paintings. Lois wrote to her sister Harriet about her proud and opinionated sister-in-law: "The truth is I cannot abide Mary and never will. I cannot tell why but there is something to me utterly obnoxious about that girl. I have never yet heard her criticize any human being in any but the most disagreeable way. She is too self-important and I can't put up with it."

During that summer, Mary Cassatt had most of her

Cassatt's *Katherine Cassatt Reading to Her Grandchildren* shows Aleck's children, *(from left)* Eddie, Elsie, and Katherine.

family with her in France: her father and mother, her sister, Lydia, and her brother's family, who spent many of their afternoons posing for her. She brought her easels and canvases outside, where she could paint in natural light. Instead of sketching imaginary scenes and then having models hold the necessary poses in her studio, she could arrange her compositions directly in front of her with her young and willing relatives.

She finished several paintings of children, including *Mother about to Wash Her Sleepy Child.* This was her first painting exploring the close emotional relationship between mothers and their children, a subject that had come to facinate her. In some of these paintings, the two figures were posed close together, with their heads almost touching and usually looking away from the viewer. She also painted a number of pictures of Lydia.

Cassatt showed several of these paintings at the sixth Impressionist exhibition in the spring of 1881. This time she risked criticism not for her painting style but for her subjects. With members of the middle class suddenly buying paintings, portraits of children and family scenes were becoming a common sight on the walls of private galleries. In fact, so many children were being painted that many critics could hardly stand to look at them. An important critic named J. K. Huysmans, however, saw something more in the paintings of Mary Cassatt and made an exception: "Oh! those babies, good heavens, how their pictures make one's hair stand on end. Such a bunch of English and French daubers have painted them in such stupid and pretentious poses! . . . Miss Cassatt, thank heavens, is not one of these daubers. . . . She achieves something that none of our painters could express, the happy contentment, the quiet friendliness of an interior."

In 1882 the Impressionists were preparing for their seventh exhibition. Once united in their battle against the Paris Salon, the artists this time were fighting among themselves. At the center of the quarrel was Edgar Degas, who wanted to exhibit the works of several of his friends at the exhibition. Claude Monet and others, however, believed these painters were not true Impressionists and did not belong in the show. When Paul Durand-Ruel, who was holding the exhibition in his gallery, insisted that only Impressionists should be included, Degas refused to take part. Out of loyalty to her friend, Mary Cassatt took Degas's side and decided not to show any of her works.

The 1882 exhibition showed that the Impressionists were moving far away from Cassatt's style of portraits and interior scenes. Monet, Renoir, and others were experimenting with light and shade and the endlessly changing appearances of water, forests, fields, the sky, and other aspects of the natural world. Fascinated by the urban world of crowds and public entertainments, Degas, Cézanne, and Sisley pictured cafés and restaurants, horse races, the theater, train stations, and the seaside. For her part, Mary Cassatt remained an indoor painter, depicting the private world of families and children at home.

For the public and for newspaper critics, the shock of the first Independents' exhibition had long worn off. Instead of ridicule, the artists now faced an even worse problem: people weren't interested. Only a few people were buying Impressionist paintings. Critics were writing about the jealousies and rivalries among the painters

Cassatt's portraits of mothers with their children show a realistic connection between the people.

instead of the artworks on display. Salon painters still held the public's attention and still dominated the market for pictures. Although many of the Independents, including Cassatt and Degas, lived well, others still had to struggle after many years of study and work.

Out of necessity, Auguste Renoir had decided to show again at the Paris Salon. He explained himself in a letter to Paul Durand-Ruel: "In Paris there are scarcely fifteen people capable of liking a painter who doesn't show at the Salon. There are 80,000 who won't buy so much as a nose from a painter who is not at the Salon. That's why I send in two portraits every year, little as that is. I send to the Salon for purely commercial reasons. Anyhow, it's like with certain medicines. If it does no good, it does no harm."

Durand-Ruel was unable to make a profit on the seventh Impressionist exhibition. In fact, his sales were so bad, and business so poor generally, that he considered closing his gallery for good. Only help from several wealthy friends, including a loan from Mary Cassatt, allowed him to stay in business.

Even as her work gained attention and buyers, Mary Cassatt found that she had less time for study and for painting. She was spending much of her time taking care of her sister, Lydia, who was suffering from a rare kidney disease. Lydia was her only sister and, like Mary, had remained single. Lydia satisfied Mary's need for companionship and support in a world that could be competitive, harsh, and uncaring. But neither Mary nor the doctors could help Lydia, and in November 1882 Lydia died.

A critic referred to *Reading Le Figaro,* Mary's portrait of her mother, as "a miracle of simplicity and elegance."

Mary's mother was ill as well, and by 1884 the illness had become serious. On the advice of a doctor, Mary and her mother traveled to Spain, where the warmer weather might help. They traveled along the Mediterranean Sea and then turned northward to the French town of Biarritz, which lay on the Atlantic Ocean. As her mother slowly

Cassatt's *Children Playing on the Beach*

recovered, Mary traveled back to Paris, where she found a new apartment for the entire family. She decided to give up her studio for a time and paint in the living room of the new apartment.

Soon after settling down, she began preparing for the Impressionist exhibition of 1886. This show would take place in a room above a restaurant on the Rue Lafitte. Mary Cassatt, Berthe Morisot and her husband, Eugène Manet, Edgar Degas, and several other artists put up the money to rent the hall and print exhibition catalogues.

Again the Impressionists were quarreling. A young painter named Georges Seurat had finished a strange and startling painting called *A Sunday on La Grande Jatte.* Seeking to develop a new, "scientific" basis for painting, Seurat had invented his own method of applying paint to canvas: Pointillism. He pressed the tip of his brush to the picture to create thousands of tiny, precise dots. The different colors of the dots combined to create large areas of flat colors.

The Impressionists could not decide whether Seurat was one of them, or even if he was a serious painter. *La Grande Jatte* fascinated painters willing to consider new methods and ideas. But to many of the Impressionists, *La Grande Jatte* was no more than a parlor trick, a work with no soul or feeling.

Mary Cassatt took little interest in these kinds of experiments. She felt herself growing apart from the new wave of painters such as Seurat, Paul Gauguin, and Henri Matisse, whom the critics were calling Neo-Impressionists or Postimpressionists. For Cassatt, the excitement of being an Independent and studying new techniques in color and composition had faded.

Camille Pissarro, who was experimenting with Seurat's new technique of Pointillism, was arguing bitterly with Eugène Manet over what to do with *A Sunday on La Grande Jatte.* Manet did not want the painting included in the exhibition, while Pissarro supported Seurat. Finally the artists agreed to show *La Grande Jatte* in a separate room with Pissarro's paintings. But the quarrel divided the Impressionists further.

That year Mary Cassatt was having her own quarrel, with Edgar Degas. Both Cassatt and Degas had sharp tongues and were expert at using a short comment or a simple gesture to dismiss painters who had no ability or whose ability didn't match their own.

Once, while visiting an exhibition, Cassatt and Degas had stopped together to view a painting. Cassatt turned to remark that the painter couldn't draw. In reply, Degas had only shrugged his shoulders: What could the painter, a woman, know about drawing?

Cassatt didn't reply. Soon afterward, she arranged for a model to come to her studio. Cassatt posed the model in front of a washstand, with one arm holding a length of hair and the other arm bent around the back of her head. The model looked away to the right, with her face in a quarter-profile. Behind her head was a jar full of water, an oval basin half hidden by one of her arms, and the corner of a mirror, reflecting the wallpaper of the room.

The artist sketched the complicated pose on the canvas, then filled it with white for the folds of the nightgown,

reddish browns for the model's hair, and darker browns
for the furniture behind her. Cassatt sent the painting to
the 1886 exhibition. As soon as he saw *Girl Arranging*

Cassatt's *Girl Arranging Her Hair*

Degas painted a portrait of Cassatt in the early 1880s. The two artists both frustrated and admired each other.

Her Hair, Edgar Degas exclaimed "What drawing!" To Cassatt's great satisfaction, he immediately decided to buy the painting himself.

Later in 1886, Paul Durand-Ruel held a show of Impressionist art at the American Art Galleries in New York. He shipped more than three hundred paintings to the United States for the show. Several paintings in the exhibition were donated by American collectors; Alexander Cassatt sent seven pictures. It was the first big Impressionist exhibition outside of Europe.

Durand-Ruel and the painters he sponsored were not sure how Americans would view Impressionist art. Only a few Impressionist paintings had ever been seen in the United States, and none had ever been shown in public galleries. All of a sudden, hundreds were being displayed all at once. Two works by Mary Cassatt were there, as well as twenty-three Degas paintings, forty-eight Monets, and thirty-eight works of Renoir.

Mary Cassatt believed that Durand-Ruel would struggle to turn a profit in the United States, just as he had struggled in France. She worried that Impressionism was too experimental for American collectors and that the critics would poke fun at this odd new European painting style. But she was wrong. Many paintings were sold, several critics praised the works, and the New York exhibition earned more than eighteen thousand dollars. After the show closed, Durand-Ruel wrote to a friend: "Don't think that the Americans are savages! On the contrary, they are less ignorant, less bound by routine than our French collectors."

In the next few years, many Americans, including Louisine Elder, began collecting Impressionist works. Louisine, who had since married a wealthy businessman and art collector named Harry Havemeyer, turned to Mary Cassatt for advice. Mary, Louisine, and Harry visited galleries in France, Italy, and Spain, where they examined and bought Impressionist paintings as well as works of Goya, Velázquez, El Greco, and painters of the Italian Renaissance.

Louisine Havemeyer and other collectors eventually donated or sold most of their works to museums in Philadelphia, New York, Chicago, Washington, and other smaller cities. Most French museums were still ignoring the works of the Impressionists, sometimes even turning down donations of works by the painters themselves. By the turn of the century, the Impressionist painters had won appreciation in their own country—but not until Durand-Ruel and other dealers had shipped hundreds of their works across the Atlantic.

7

PRINTMAKING

In 1890 Mary Cassatt and her parents rented a house in the small village of Bachivillers. There Mary set up a small studio with a printing press where she could work on printmaking in the evenings, after the outdoor light was gone.

While studying in Italy, she had learned from Carlo Raimondi that there were many different ways to create a print. Each method posed a different challenge to the artist; each created a different effect of line and color. But all demanded skill, precision, and many hours of hard work. The artist had to work as carefully as possible—once a line was made in the printer's plate, it could not be erased, changed, or covered.

Like other artists, Cassatt made drypoint engravings by cutting lines in flat copper plates with a sharp steel tool

Cassatt's lithograph of a mother and child shows a banjo lesson.

called a burin. As the burin was pushed across the plate, it cut a V-shaped groove in the metal and threw up a long, thin fragment of copper, called a burr, along the sides of the groove. After clearing the burr off the plate, Cassatt spread ink on the plate with a roller or applied the ink with a small piece of felt. The plate was then run through a press, transferring the drawing to a sheet of paper. Copper was soft enough to cut but hard enough to keep its shape in the press; for this reason several hundred prints could sometimes be "pulled" from the same plate.

Cassatt also worked at soft-ground etching, in which she spread a soft wax or thin varnish on the copper plate to make a "ground." She then placed a thin piece of paper over the plate and used a tool to draw lines on the paper. Where she had drawn the lines, the ground stuck to the back of the paper and then came off the plate when the paper was removed. She dipped the plate in acid, which etched into the exposed lines. Then she inked different areas of the plate with different colors. To do this, she used small, bunched-up rags to apply the colors. She called this *à la poupée,* meaning "with dolls," because the rags reminded her of little dolls. Finally, she pressed the finished plate against a sheet of paper to create a print.

Cassatt transferred many of the new techniques of Impressionist painting to her prints. She placed strong colors side by side to create new effects. She blurred or focused lines to bring out certain features of the scene or the models. Areas of solid color were contrasted with areas of complicated patterns. In a series of prints, slightly different shades of ink could be used. This allowed a large range of colors that nearly matched those of an oil painting.

Cassatt bought many prints to study and always attended important exhibitions. In the spring of 1890, the École des Beaux-Arts in Paris exhibited more than seven hundred Japanese *ukiyo-e* prints, boldly colored scenes of everyday life in Japan. Traditional ukiyo-e depicted the world of theater, dancers, and other entertainments; others were portraits of nobles or samurai warriors, or dramatic landscapes of forests, mountains, and streams. Ukiyo-e prints revealed a world entirely foreign to Europeans and offered Impressionist artists new techniques of design and color.

The Japanese artists had created their prints by carving designs into blocks of wood, then inking the wood and pressing it against paper. For each color in the print, a different block of wood was used. The paper was sometimes passed over several different blocks before the print was finished. Instead of filling their pictures with detailed, complex compositions, Japanese artists combined simple lines and unusual perspectives. A beautifully drawn line or a subtle curve might suggest a range of mountains or a distant forest. Large areas of the prints were covered by a strong, primary color, juxtaposed against other areas of complex patterns and design. Other areas were left blank, to highlight and contrast space occupied by the subject.

The French were soon buying shiploads of Japanese pottery, lacquerware, painted screens, fans, and household objects. La Porte Chinoise, a shop on the Rue de Rivoli in Paris, attracted many of the Impressionist

One of Utagawa Kunisada's prints shows an engraver and a printer making prints.

painters; Degas and Monet bought hundreds of prints at this shop and others like it. A bridge he had seen in a Japanese print inspired Monet to design a similar bridge at his home in Giverny; he spent much of the rest of his life sketching and painting the bridge and the small lily pond it crossed.

The exhibition of 1890 inspired Mary Cassatt to work on a new series of color prints using three techniques she

Monet painted his Japanese bridge at many different times of day and in different seasons.

had learned: drypoint, soft-ground etching, and aquatint. In aquatint, Cassatt coated the surface of a copper plate with a resin and then carefully painted it with colored ink. She used drypoint for the lines of the drawing, soft-ground etching for areas of color, and the aquatint method for color backgrounds and patterns in clothing and wall-paper. Each step had to be carefully planned.

Cassatt experimented with new color effects in her prints. Imitating the woodblock technique of Japanese printmakers, she prepared several plates, one for each color to appear in the print. The different plates were sent through a printing press to create the final print. The work was long and difficult; Cassatt had to work many hours at her small printer's shop to finish only a few proofs.

In a series of ten prints she completed in early 1891, Cassatt depicted women in their homes doing everyday things such as sending letters, washing, or taking care of children. Cassatt tried to depict difficult poses and com-positions with simple lines. In *The Fitting,* a woman tries a new dress while standing in front of a mirror. Another woman kneels in the bottom half of the print, with her back to the viewer. A reflection in a tall mirror forms a third figure, posed as if looking away into the distance.

The 1890 exhibition in Paris had sparked public interest in printmaking techniques. In 1891 the Impressionists pre-pared an exhibit of prints created by their members. But the members of the group laid down a new rule—those who were not French citizens would not be admitted. The rule excluded Mary Cassatt as well as Camille Pissarro, who had been born in the Dutch West Indies.

Cassatt and Pissarro protested with an exhibition of their works in a gallery right next door, which angered many of the artists exhibiting with the French group.

Cassatt's print, *The Bath,* shows an interest in textile patterns similar to those in Japanese ukiyo-e prints.

Although Cassatt's print *On the Bus* shows two women and a child in a public setting, the focus on the three people is still intimate.

Cassatt's exclusion also inspired her to put on her first solo exhibition, to be held at Paul Durand-Ruel's gallery. She showed two pastel drawings, two paintings, and ten color prints. Interested critics and eager buyers crowded both shows. Many artists who saw her prints believed them to be her best works. When he saw an aquatint entitled *Woman Bathing,* Degas exclaimed, "I won't admit that a woman can draw like that!"

Others were still critical of Mary Cassatt's works; none of her works hanging in the Durand-Ruel gallery were sold. To many critics and buyers, she was a talented but limited artist who only worked with a single subject. There was a fine sentiment in the world of mothers and children, but there was much more to the world than mothers and children. Art was changing with a fast-moving world, and painters were following the events closely with innovations of their own. Cassatt painted only comfortable domestic life; she ignored the city and its crowds, she knew nothing about the world of workers or farmers. The era of industry, science, and progress had escaped her notice.

Seurat and other Neo-Impressionists, as they were called, were making new innovations in painting style. The Impressionists, meanwhile, had grown older. Though they had once been independent, their works had become traditional and acceptable. Hundreds of artists with less talent were imitating the Impressionists' landscapes and city scenes. Painting styles seemed to change in the same way as clothing, hats, and shoes; and the new fashion in painting was leaving Cassatt, Degas, and their colleagues behind.

8

A MORE TRADITIONAL CHALLENGE

To Mary Cassatt, painting and printmaking were important. They were much more important than marrying and raising a family. But she had stayed close to her brothers and their parents, often living with them. During the summers, Mary and her parents lived in a *château,* or manor house, they rented in the small village of Bachivillers. It was a big, quiet country home with surrounding fields and gardens. There were no noisy distractions, as in the big city of Paris, and fewer visitors. In Bachivillers, Mary could work all day long without interruptions.

Her parents' well-being still occupied much of her time. Robert Cassatt's health had been gradually failing, and in December 1891, he died in Paris. Both Mary and her mother lost a friend who had often helped them with advice and reassurance. Soon afterward, Mary began looking for a permanent house of her own, where she could settle down and provide a quiet and comfortable

Cassatt's unsentimental portraits of ordinary mothers and their young children gave her a reputation as a modern artist.

life for herself and her mother. The sadness over her father's death would be helped by traveling with her mother, her brother Gard's wife, Jennie, and her nephew Gard in the South of France.

When Mary returned to Paris in the spring of 1892, officials from the World's Columbian Exposition in Chicago, a huge fair of science and invention, asked her to paint a mural for one of the high walls of the Woman's Building. The building was designed by a female architect; it would be decorated by female artists and would hold exhibits of female inventions and designs. The officials wanted two large murals: one entitled *Primitive Woman* and the other entitled *Modern Woman.* Together the murals would show the great progress and achievements women had made in the modern world. The officials had already decided on a traditional academic painter, Mary MacMonnies, to do *Primitive Woman.* For *Modern Woman,* they hired Mary Cassatt.

Mary had to think this commission over carefully. She had never worked on such a huge canvas—twelve feet high by fifty-eight feet long—and she had never done a mural of any kind. She had spent most of her life breaking away from tradition, and decorating a wall with a "theme" for a world's fair was very traditional. Painting a mural was like designing wallpaper—in order to be good, the mural had to blend in with the design of the room where it would be shown. Such a project wouldn't interest the Impressionists, who liked to express their feelings and visions as independently as possible. But when Mary's old friend and rival Edgar Degas showed contempt for such a project, she took it on with enthusiasm. She described the scene to a friend: "The bare idea of such a thing put Degas in a rage . . . I got my spirit up and said I would not give up the idea for anything."

The mural contained three separate paintings. As in many of the academic pictures she had studied as a student, the figures in her mural were used as symbols. They stood for Fame, Music, and Science. In the central panel, women are plucking fruit from a tree, symbolizing science and knowledge. On the left, women are chasing after a figure that symbolizes fame. Three geese, symbolizing critics, honk and snap at the women's feet. On the right, one woman plays a banjo while another dances. A three-foot-wide decorative border surrounded each painting in the mural.

To complete the mural, Cassatt worked in a tall, glass-roofed studio on the grounds of the château in Bachivillers. She set up the paintings inside the studio. Workmen dug a trench sixty feet long and six feet deep into the ground. When she had to work on the topmost portions of the paintings, workmen lowered the paintings into the ground. No ladder was necessary!

The mural was the most difficult work Cassatt had ever done. Its sheer size made it difficult to judge, and she nearly asked her old friend Degas to come up to the studio to have a look. "But if he happens to be in the mood," she wrote to a friend, "he would demolish me so completely that I could never pick myself up in time to finish." Finally, and just in time, she finished the work and had it shipped by boat and then train to Chicago. When it was put in place for the exposition in the spring of 1893, the mural stood nearly fifty feet off the ground. But the strong colors seemed harsh and unpleasant high on the wall, and the symbolic themes of the paintings mystified fairgoers and displeased critics. After the Columbian Exposition closed, the organizers of the exposition put the mural into storage, and it has since disappeared.

Mary was pleased with her work on the project, despite its many problems, and she paid little attention to critical notices in American newspapers. After the work on the Chicago mural was finished, Cassatt prepared another solo exhibition for Durand-Ruel's gallery in Paris. The

Cassatt's *The Bath*

exhibition took place in November 1893 and included ninety-eight works. One of the works hung at the exhibition was *The Bath,* a picture that shows a woman holding a child in her lap and washing the child's feet in a small basin. The picture has a strong design, careful balance of colors, and very precise drawing. Many critics greatly admired *The Bath* at the 1893 show, and the painting became the most famous Mary Cassatt ever did.

In 1894, after years of renting summer homes with her parents, Mary bought a house, the Château de Beaufresne. Beaufresne lay on a hill near the village of Mesnil-Théribus, about five miles from Bachivillers. Forests, hills, and small fields surrounded the château, an old manor house built in the seventeenth century. Many small French villages had just such a large house that had once belonged to a local noble or a wealthy landowner. Beaufresne itself had once been used as a royal hunting lodge.

Cassatt set many paintings, including *Family Group—Reading,* on the grounds of her new home.

Forty-five acres of grounds surrounded the house. A narrow stream fed a small pond on the west side of the house, where chestnut and willow trees grew along the edges of a wide green lawn. Two six-sided towers rose on each side of the house in front. Rows of windows lined the lower two stories. On the first floor were an oval dining room, a parlor, and a glass arcade. On the second and third floors were smaller rooms and bedrooms.

Beaufresne was big but in bad repair. The bathrooms and hallways needed new paint, the walls new plaster, and the roof new slate shingles. Mary had a gardener build new walkways, plant vegetable gardens, and tend to small

The Château de Beaufresne

fruit orchards. She also had more than a thousand rose bushes planted on the grounds. In 1895, after nearly two years of work, Cassatt and her mother moved in with a cook, a gardener, a chambermaid, and a coachman, who would soon learn to drive a new motorcar.

A few months after Mary and her mother moved into the château, Katherine Cassatt died. Bereft by the loss of her mother, Mary counted on the comfort of Louisine Havemeyer, who came to France to spend time with her friend. Over the years, many other friends also visited, as did her brothers with their families, other artists, journalists, art students, and politicians.

The grounds of the château made a fine setting for many paintings. Cassatt worked outside on the grounds or in the glass arcade at the back of the house that looked out over the willow trees and ponds. She often hired local women and their children as models, posing them on the property. Instead of showing the indoor light of a painting studio, these pictures show the bright light of a sunny afternoon or the flat light of the overcast days that were common in the spring and fall.

9

FAME AND HONOR

Miss Mary Cassatt, sister of President Cassatt of the
Pennsylvania Railroad, returned from Europe yesterday.
She has been studying painting in France and owns
the smallest Pekingese dog in the world.
—The Philadelphia Ledger

Mary had again braved the wind and waves of the Atlantic Ocean to return to Philadelphia in 1898. Although many newspapers, such as the *Ledger,* still did not take her seriously as an artist, she had sold many of her paintings in Philadelphia and in New York. After Paul Durand-Ruel had held a successful one-woman exhibition of her work at his New York gallery in April 1895, art dealers promoted Mary Cassatt as the leading American member of the Impressionist school. Critics ranked her with other leading American artists: Winslow Homer, James McNeill Whistler, and John Singer Sargent.

Like Mary Cassatt, many of these artists had left the

Cassatt's *Sara in a Green Bonnet*

United States to study painting in European ateliers. Although they had taken up some elements of Impressionism, they had held closely to their academic lessons in color and composition. Meanwhile, Impressionism had

Mary Cassatt always kept up-to-date by reading newspapers and books and by holding intellectual conversations with friends and visitors.

interested few painters working in the United States until the late nineteenth century. By that time, young European artists were replacing Impressionism with entirely new painting styles.

Mary Cassatt spent much of her time helping museums in the United States buy Impressionist works for their collections. Some day, she knew, these paintings would be an important part of art history, and she would make sure they found a home in her own country. The Metropolitan Museum of Art in New York, as well as large public museums in Chicago, Philadelphia, Boston, and Washington, gathered important Impressionist works thanks to Cassatt and the collectors she helped and advised.

As if to return the favor, museums in the United States were finally recognizing Mary Cassatt as a woman of great talent. In 1904 the Pennsylvania Academy of Fine Arts awarded her a prize of three hundred dollars for a painting called *The Caress.* The painting showed a child in its mother's arms with an older girl standing alongside. The pools and lawns of Beaufresne formed the background. The woman was dressed in rich velvet, and the girl was kissing the child. The Academy, which owned the painting, would show *The Caress* in a place of honor for its seventy-third annual exhibition.

Cassatt did not forget her Impressionist principles, however. There should be no awards for paintings! She wrote a polite letter to the Academy: "I, however, who belong to the founders of the Independent Exhibition, must stick to my principles, which were no jury, no medals, no awards. Liberty is the first good in this world

Cassatt's *The Caress*

and to escape the tyranny of a jury is worth fighting for."

The same painting won another prize from the Art Institute of Chicago, in the amount of five hundred dollars. Instead of accepting the money, Cassatt donated it to an artist named Alan Philbrick, who like Mary Cassatt many years earlier was a young artist studying on his own in Europe.

In 1904 the French government named Mary Cassatt a Chevalier de la Légion d'Honneur. This award honored people who had made great achievements in many different fields: art, politics, science, sports, literature. The Légion d'Honneur came in the form of a medal and a red ribbon, and was awarded at a grand ceremony in Paris. Since it carried no money and was not a competition, Cassatt decided to accept it. Following tradition, she wore the ribbon for a full year after receiving the award.

Cassatt worked every day—outside in good weather, indoors when it rained. She worked on dozens of paintings and pastel drawings in the gardens and studio of

On the ground floor in the back of the château, Cassatt painted in her sun-drenched studio.

Beaufresne. She often asked women from Mesnil-Théribus and other nearby villages to model with their children, posing them in boats in the pond or underneath the trees in the orchard.

Cassatt's style had changed little since the 1890s. Once a radical member of a revolutionary art movement, she

Cassatt's *The Crocheting Lesson,* a drypoint print, shows a local woman and her daughter.

seemed to have become careful and conservative. While the subject matter of her pictures remained the same, the complex compositions disappeared. Lines lost their sharpness; the palette of colors she used grew limited. Many of her works were simple portraits, with backgrounds of flat color and little detail in the clothing, faces, or settings. They were reminiscent of her early Salon paintings, in which the figures were larger and heavier and more richly dressed.

She often traveled to Paris to see friends or to visit art galleries, which were selling Impressionist works by the hundreds. Paul Durand-Ruel exhibited and sold dozens of her works to eager buyers from France and the United States who recognized her as one of the best female artists in either country. Reviewers called her "the most eminent of American women painters."

Riding in a fine carriage or in her new Renault car, she also went down to Paris to view the works of younger painters who, like the Impressionists before them, were angering critics and shocking the public. In Cubism, a radical new style, these painters broke their figures and objects into irregular geometric shapes, filled with solid blocks of color. The subject could scarcely be recognized in a Cubist painting. Instead, the viewer could see only an irregular pattern of colors that resembled a reflection seen in a shattered mirror.

Mary Cassatt had not changed her own style, and she didn't care much for Cubism or any other new painting method. She disliked the works of Georges Braque and Pablo Picasso, the best known young Cubists, and wouldn't recommend them to her friends who collected paintings. She believed that Cubist painters had no ability, as they couldn't show objects as they really appeared. They had no sense of design or color. Cubist painting was done for the sake of scandal and notoriety, to attract attention. She was sure that it wouldn't last.

Even painters of her own generation bewildered her. She could not appreciate the latest works of Paul Cézanne; the subjects of his still lifes and landscapes were broken up into small blocks of solid colors. She also disliked the paintings Claude Monet had done in his garden at Giverny. His plants, gardens, and ponds seemed to float across the canvas in a mist of blue and green paint. The viewer could recognize little from the real world; instead, Monet's paintings only suggested the sight of a garden. To those who admired the works, Monet and Cézanne's ways of expressing colors and moods took Impressionist techniques in a new and fascinating direction. To Mary Cassatt, their works looked like wallpaper.

One evening, a friend drove her to the apartment of a writer named Michael Stein, who had collected many modern paintings in his home. Cassatt spent a few moments closely examining the other guests and the art. One of the artists present was Henri Matisse, who had begun painting in an Impressionist style and then had switched to a new technique of his own. Matisse earned praise from all the guests except Mary Cassatt. In a voice carrying all her pride and independence, she proclaimed: "I have never in my life seen so many dreadful people, and so many dreadful paintings, in one place!"

As Mary Cassatt grew older, her eyesight began to weaken. She had spent thousands of hours working by the weak oil and gas lamps of painting studios. But even working by daylight shining through the glass-ceilinged atelier at Beaufresne became difficult. In 1910, for a change of scenery, Mary took a long voyage with her brother Gardner and his family through eastern Europe and the Middle East. The group boarded a boat for a trip along the Nile River and stopped to visit the pyramids and

Mary joined Gard's family for a trip to Egypt.

the gigantic ancient temples at Cairo, Luxor, and Aswan. Mary had always been a hardy, enthusiastic traveler. But the hot climate, strange surroundings, and massive buildings made her feel weak, almost powerless. Worse, Gardner came down with a serious illness, and soon after returning from the trip, he died. With the death of Gardner, Mary had lost the last member of her immediate family.

Around 1912 cataracts on her eyes began to cloud her vision. She had to give up printmaking. She worked only with pastel crayons, which didn't need to be carefully mixed liked oil paints. By 1914 she stopped painting entirely. Degas, her close friend who had first invited her to exhibit with the Independents, was also suffering poor eyesight. As the years passed, he had grown into a bitter and lonely old man.

In 1915 Louisine Havemeyer put on a joint exhibition of Degas and Cassatt's works in New York to benefit the suffrage movement, which sought to give women the right to vote. The exhibit was a success, but Mary's sisters-in-law and nieces and nephews didn't attend, as they didn't believe women should have the vote. Mary was appalled at their lack of respect for women and for her, and she began to sell or give away the paintings she had been saving for her heirs.

In 1917 Cassatt's old friend Edgar Degas grew sick and died. Meanwhile, World War I raged in northern France. Several times Mary Cassatt had to leave her house and move to southern France to escape the war. She grew lonely and with her failing eyesight could barely write letters to the friends and relatives who were still alive.

Mary Cassatt walks through her gardens at Beaufresne.

She began to forget familiar people and grew quarrelsome with her old friends. When her maid found old copper drypoint printing plates in a closet, Cassatt had the plates printed and sent the prints to the Metropolitan Museum in New York. But Louisine Havemeyer recognized the prints as something the museum already owned, so she advised the museum's director not to buy them. This greatly angered Mary Cassatt, who thought Louisine was accusing everyone involved of dishonesty. Mary did not write to her friend for months. Later, it was discovered that a few of the plates had not been printed before.

Doctors operated on Cassatt's eyes to remove her cataracts, but the operations failed, and in the 1920s, she went completely blind. Diabetes and other illnesses kept her in bed for long periods of time. She died on June 14, 1926. To honor her as a Chevalier de la Légion d'Honneur, the villagers of Mesnil-Théribus held a long procession through the streets of town, from the Château de Beaufresne up a small hill to the village cemetery. There she was buried in a family tomb, where her father, mother, her sister, Lydia, and her brother Robert had also been laid to rest.

Important Impressionist Artists

Paul Cézanne (1839–1906) was born in Aix-en-Provence, a town in southern France. Many of his paintings were rejected by the Salon. In the 1870s, he exhibited twice with the Impressionists. Later he moved to Provence, studying for nearly twenty years until exhibiting his works again in 1895. His most famous works are still lifes and a series of outdoor paintings of the Mont Sainte-Victoire in Provence.

Edgar Degas (1834–1917) studied law before taking up the study of painting in the atelier of the artist Barrias. He joined the French army during the Franco-Prussian War. After the war, he participated in the Impressionist exhibitions in Paris. He held his only solo exhibition at Durand-Ruel's gallery in 1893. In later years, he devoted himself mainly to sculpture.

Édouard Manet (1832–1883) was born into a wealthy family and spent many hours studying Italian and Spanish painting in the halls of the Louvre. He fought against academic painting with pictures—*Luncheon on the Grass* and *Olympia*—that scandalized the art world in the 1860s. Yet he never exhibited with the Impressionists, believing that the Paris Salon was the best place to fight traditional art.

Claude Monet (1840–1926) grew up in the port of Le Havre and moved to Paris when he was nineteen. Many of his paintings are studies in the changing properties of sunlight and shadow. He completed more than fifty studies of light on the face of the cathedral of Rouen. In 1883 he moved to a country house in the village of Giverny. His paintings found a large market, and he became famous and wealthy in the 1880s.

Berthe Morisot (1841–1895) was born in Bourges, in central France, and studied painting in Paris with Camille Corot during the 1860s. She regularly exhibited her paintings at the Paris Salon but later joined the Impressionist movement under the influence of Édouard Manet, the brother of her husband, Eugène.

Camille Pissarro (1830–1903) was born in St. Thomas, in the Caribbean, and moved to Paris when he was twenty-five. He joined the Impressionists in the 1870s and exhibited at all eight of their shows. His paintings of village life and of nature combine careful composition and a wide palette of realistic, natural colors.

Auguste Renoir (1841–1919) was born in Limoges but grew up in Paris, where he worked in a porcelain factory as a young man. He painted many outdoor scenes and exhibited at the Paris Salon as well as with the Impressionists. He suffered from arthritis and, in his last few years, had to attach the paintbrush to his hands in order to work.

WHERE TO SEE SOME OF THE PAINTINGS OF MARY CASSATT AND OTHER IMPRESSIONISTS

Musée d'Orsay, Paris
Cézanne: *Les Joueurs de Cartes*
Degas: *À la Bourse*
L'Absinthe
La Danseuse Étoile
Manet: *Le Déjeuner sur l'Herbe (Luncheon on the Grass)*
Olympia

Musée Marmottan, Paris
Monet: *Impression, Soleil Levant (Impression, Sunrise)*

Museum of Fine Arts, Boston
Cassatt: *At the Opera*
Five O'Clock Tea

The Art Institute of Chicago
Cassatt: *The Bath*
Toreador
Cézanne: *The Basket of Apples*
The Bay of Marseilles
Degas: *Ballet at the Paris Opera*
The Millinery Shop
Manet: *Courses à Longchamp*
Fish (Still Life)
The Mocking of Christ
Monet: *Arrival of the Normandy Train, Saint-Lazare Station*
Grainstacks (End of Summer)
Water Lilies
Morisot: *Woman at Her Toilette*
Renoir: *Jugglers at the Circus Fernando*
Two Sisters (On the Terrace)
Seurat: *A Sunday on La Grande Jatte*

Metropolitan Museum of Art, New York
Cassatt: *Lady at the Tea Table*
    Self-Portrait
Degas: *Mary Cassatt in the Louvre*
    The Rehearsal of the Ballet Onstage

Philadelphia Museum of Art
Cassatt: *Family Group—Reading*
    Mary Ellison Embroidering
    On the Balcony
    Portrait of Alexander J. Cassatt, and His Son, Robert Kelso
    Woman with a Pearl Necklace in a Loge
Cézanne: *Les Grandes Baigneuses*

National Gallery of Art, Washington, D.C.
Cassatt: *Children Playing on the Beach*
    The Fitting
    Girl Arranging Her Hair
    Little Girl in a Blue Armchair
    The Loge
Cézanne: *The Artist's Father*
Degas: *Ballet Dancers*
    Before the Ballet
    Dancers Backstage
    Madame René de Gas
Manet: *Gare Saint-Lazare*
    Le Bal Masqué à l'Opéra
    The Old Musician
Monet: *Argenteuil*
    The Artist's Garden at Vétheuil
    Rouen Cathedral, West Facade, Sunlight
    Rouen Cathedral, West Facade
Renoir: *A Girl with a Watering Can*
    Le Pont-Neuf

Smithsonian Institution, Washington D.C.
Degas: *Mary Cassatt*

BIBLIOGRAPHY

Bullard, E. John. *Mary Cassatt: Oils and Pastels.* New York: Watson-Guptill, 1972.

Carson, Julie. *Mary Cassatt.* New York: David McKay, 1966.

Costantino, Maria. *Mary Cassatt.* Greenwich, CT: Brompton Books, 1995.

Hale, Nancy. *Mary Cassatt.* New York: Doubleday, 1975.

Mary Cassatt: Pastels and Color Prints. Washington, DC: Smithsonian Institution Press, 1978.

Mathews, Nancy Mowll. *Mary Cassatt: A Life.* New York: Villard Books, 1994.

Salvi, Francesco. *Les Impressionistes.* Paris: Hatier, 1994.

Sweet, Frederick A. *Miss Mary Cassatt: Impressionist from Pennsylvania.* Norman, OK: University of Oklahoma Press, 1966.

INDEX

(Numbers in **bold** refer to illustrations.)

academic painting. *See* Paris Salon; traditional approach to painting
At the Opera, 55–**56**

Bath, The, **88,** 89
Bath, The, (print), **81**

Caress, The, 95, **96**
Cassatt, Alexander (brother), 7, 12, 13, 14, 28, 58, **60,** 61, 72, 92
Cassatt, Gardner (brother), 7, **11,** 85, **101,** 102
Cassatt, Jennie (sister-in-law), 85, **101,** 102
Cassatt, Katherine (mother), 7, 22, 28, 54, **61,** 62, **66**–67, 74, 84–85, 91, 104
Cassatt, Lois Buchanan (sister-in-law), 28, 60, 61, 102
Cassatt, Lydia (sister), 7, 13, 44, **53,** 54, 55, **57,** 62, 65, 104
Cassatt, Mary: **11, 20, 31, 51, 52, 59, 71, 94, 101, 103;** approach to painting, 14–15, 32–33, 44–45, 55, 62–63, 69–70, 86–87, 91; approach to printmaking, 74–77, 80; awards, 95–97; birth of, 8; commissioned paintings, 30–32, 45–**46;** critics' reaction to, 53, 54, 55, 62–63, 83; determination of, 15–16, 21, 45, 55, 84; first solo exhibition, 83; observations of, 6, 9–10; paintings by *(see under specific titles)*

Cassatt, Robert (brother), 7, **11,** 12, 104
Cassatt, Robert (father), 7, 8–9, **11,** 12, 13, 15–16, 21, 54, 62, 74, 84, 104
Cézanne, Paul, 40–41, 63, 100
Château de Beaufresne, 89, **90,** 91, **97,** 101, **103,** 104
Child in His Mother's Arms, **85**
Children Playing on the Beach, **67**
collecting art, 38, 58, 64, 72–73, 95
colors, use of, in art, 15, 18, 32–33, 37, 76–77, 80, 99
composition in art, 14, 16, 18–19, 32, 44–45, 48, 55, 62, 69–70, 76–77
Crocheting Lesson, The, **98**
Cubism, 99–100

Degas, Edgar, 37–38, 39, 41, 47–49, **50,** 51, 63, 68, 69, 70–71, 79, 83, 102; *Ballet Rehearsal,* 37–38; *The Bathers,* 41; *Mary Cassatt,* **71;** *Mary Cassatt in the Louvre,* **51;** *The Rehearsal of the Ballet Onstage,* **38**
Delacroix, Eugène, 12–13
Durand-Ruel, Paul, 54–55, 63, 65, 72, 73, 83, 87, 92

Elder, Louisine. *See* Havemeyer, Louisine
engraving, 33, 74–76, **78,** 80, 98
Exposition Universelle, 12–13

Family Group—Reading, **89**
Fitting, The, 80
Five O'Clock Tea, **57**

Girl Arranging Her Hair, 69, **70,** 71

Haldeman, Eliza, **20,** 22, 26, 27, 58

Havemeyer, Louisine, 37, 38, 46, 58, 72–73, 91, 102, 104
Homer, Winslow, 92; *Art Students and Copyists in the Louvre Gallery,* **25**

Ida, 39, 44
Impressionists, 41–44, 47–48, 50, 51, 63–65, 68–69, 80–82, 83, 95; approach to painting, 41–43, 63, 83, 100; definition of, 43; exhibitions, 44, 47, 50–51, 62, 63, 68, 72, 80–81

Japanese printmaking, 77, **78,** 79, 81

Katherine Cassatt Reading to Her Grandchildren, **61**
Kunisada, Utagawa, *Different Processes of Printmaking,* **78**

Little Girl in a Blue Armchair, **49**
Louvre, **25, 51**

Manet, Édouard, 27, 41; *Balcony, The,* 34, **35**; *Luncheon on the Grass,* 27, 41;
Manet, Eugène, 68, 69
Mary Ellison Embroidering, **46**
Modern Woman, 86–87
Monet, Claude, 41, 44, 51, 63, 72, 79, 100; *Impression, Sunrise,* **43;** *Japanese Bridge over the Lilacs Pond at Giverny,* **79**
Morisot, Berthe, **35,** 41, 68
Mother about to Wash Her Sleepy Child, 62
Mother and Child, **64**
Mother and Child (lithograph), **75**

Neo–Impressionists, 68–69, 83

On the Balcony, 33–**34,** 36
On the Bus, **82**

Paris, life in, 9–11, 22–26, **42,** 44
Paris Salon, 23–**24,** 26, 28, 34, 36, 38–39, 40–45, 65
Pennsylvania, life in, 8, 14
Pennsylvania Academy of Fine Arts, 16–21, 54, 95
Pissarro, Camille, 41, 44, 69, 81–82; *Boulevard Montmartre in Paris,* **42**
Pointillism, 68, 69
Portrait of Alexander J. Cassatt, and His Son, Robert Kelso Cassatt, **60**

Reading Le Figaro, **66**
Renoir, Auguste, 41, 44, 63, 65, 72

Sara in a Green Bonnet, **93**
Sartain, Emily, 30, 48, 59
Self-Portrait, **52**
Self-Portrait (watercolor), **59**
Seurat, Georges, 68–69, 83; *A Sunday on La Grande Jatte,* 68–69
Sisley, Alfred, 41, 44, 63

Tourny, Léon, 37, 39, 48
traditional approach to painting, 14–15, 16–20, 23–26, 30–34, 36–37, 41, 93. *See also* Paris Salon

Woman Bathing, 83
Woman with a Pearl Necklace in a Loge, **53**

ACKNOWLEDGMENTS

Cover illustration by Lejla Fazlic Omerovic.

Text illustrations are reprinted with the permission of: Frederick A. Sweet Papers, Archives of American Art, Smithsonian Institution, pp. 2, 90, 97, 101; The Historical Society of Pennsylvania, p. 7; Peter Baumgärtner, *Robert Cassatt and His Children,* 1854, IPS, p. 11; Art Resource, NY: (Snark) p. 13, (Erich Lessing) p. 35, (Scala) pp. 42, 88, (Giraudon) pp. 43, 64, 79, 82, 85, (National Portrait Gallery, Smithsonian Institution) pp. 59, 71, (Victoria and Albert Museum, London) pp. 78, 98, (Art Resource) p. 81, (National Museum of American Art, Washington, DC) pp. 93, 96; Pennsylvania Academy of the Fine Arts, Philadelphia, Archives, pp. 17, 20, 31; Bibliothèque Nationale, pp. 24, 50; Corbis–Bettmann, p. 25; Cassatt, *On the Balcony,* Philadelphia Museum of Art: W.P. Wilstach Collection, p. 34; Degas, *The Rehearsal of the Ballet Onstage,* Metropolitan Museum of Art, H.O. Havemeyer Collection, Gift of Horace Havemeyer, 1929, (29.160.26), p. 38; Cassatt, *Mary Ellison Embroidering,* Philadelphia Museum of Art: Gift of the Children of Jena Thompson Thayer, p. 46; Cassatt, *Little Girl in a Blue Armchair,* National Gallery of Art, Washington, Collection of Mr. and Mrs. Paul Mellon, p. 49; Degas, *Mary Cassatt in the Louvre, Museum of Antiquities,* Metropolitan Museum of Art, Rogers Fund, 1919, (19.29.2), p. 51; Cassatt, *Self–Portrait,* Metropolitan Museum of Art, Bequest of Edith H. Proskauer, 1975, (1975.319.1), p. 52; Cassatt, *Woman with a Pearl Necklace in a Loge,* Philadelphia Museum of Art: Bequest of Charlotte Dorrance Wright, p. 53; Cassatt, *At the Opera,* Museum of Fine Arts, Boston, The Hayden Collection, p. 56; Cassatt, *The Tea,* Museum of Fine Arts, Boston, M. Theresa B. Hopkins Fund, p. 57; Cassatt, *Portrait of Alexander J. Cassatt, and His Son, Robert Kelso Cassatt,* Philadelphia Museum of Art: Purchased with the W.P. Wilstach Fund and Funds Contributed by Mrs. William Coxe Wright, p. 60; Cassatt, *Grandmother Reading to Children,* Private Collection, New York/Bridgeman Art Library, London/New York, p. 61; Cassatt, *Reading Le Figaro,* Christie's Images/Bridgeman Art Library, London/New York, p. 66; Cassatt, *Children Playing on the Beach,* National Gallery of Art, Washington, Ailsa Mellon Bruce Collection, p. 67; Cassatt, *Girl Arranging Her Hair,* National Gallery of Art, Washington, Chester Dale Collection, p. 70; Cassatt, *Mother and Child* (litho), Agnew and Sons, London, UK/Bridgeman Art Library, London/New York, p. 75; Cassatt, *Family Group–Reading,* Philadelphia Museum of Art: Given by Mr. and Mrs. J. Watson Webb, p. 89; Hill–Stead Museum, pp. 94, 103.